To
John + Beverly
Warm Wishes
Lillian Carter
Oct., 1981

BRIDGES

by

LILLIAN C. CANZLER

Clark Canzler Books • Ellensburg, Washington

Dedicated to my grandchildren.

Copyright ©1986 by Lillian C. Canzler
Published by Clark Canzler Books
5121 So. Mead, Seattle, WA 98118
Printed by Hancock Printing Service
Ellensburg, Washington 98926

ISBN 0-941769-00-3

ACKNOWLEDGEMENTS:

Without the constant help and support of my husband, David, and his trusty sailboat, Lilith, this book could not have been produced.

Si Wei-Hong and Ma Hong-Gang, Hefei, China, translated the book into Chinese dialects.

Seattle Times, picture of bridge in a storm, page 37.

The bridges in this book are found in the United States of America in the states of Washington and Oregon.

This is a book about bridges. Bridges are structures that are built to provide passage over obstacles like ditches, rivers, railroads, or freeways.

Bridges come in many different sizes and styles.

Some bridges span deep canyons.

Some bridges cross wide rivers.

Complex freeways include many bridges.

One simple bridge may cross a small creek

or
a high
mountain
stream.

Two bridges, together, may look like twins.

13

Bridges allow men, women, and children to cross on them.

On large bridges, people ride bicycles and motorcycles.
Some people walk and many others ride in cars and buses.

Narrow,
hanging bridges allow
only foot traffic.

Have you ever walked on a hanging bridge?

Sometimes there are problems with bridges. People want to walk or drive over them and boats with high masts want to sail under them. Some bridges can separate in the middle and lift up to allow boats to sail under them. The people on top must wait until the bridge moves back together again.

Taller bridges allow boats to glide under while people in cars ride over them.

When bridges become old, or traffic is too heavy, new bridges are built.

Can you find the old bridge in this picture?

Building new bridges is exciting, courageous work for both men and women.

Stop! Pay! You're on a new bridge.

Now you are on a
bridge being painted
to look like new.

Not all bridges are replaced when they become old.

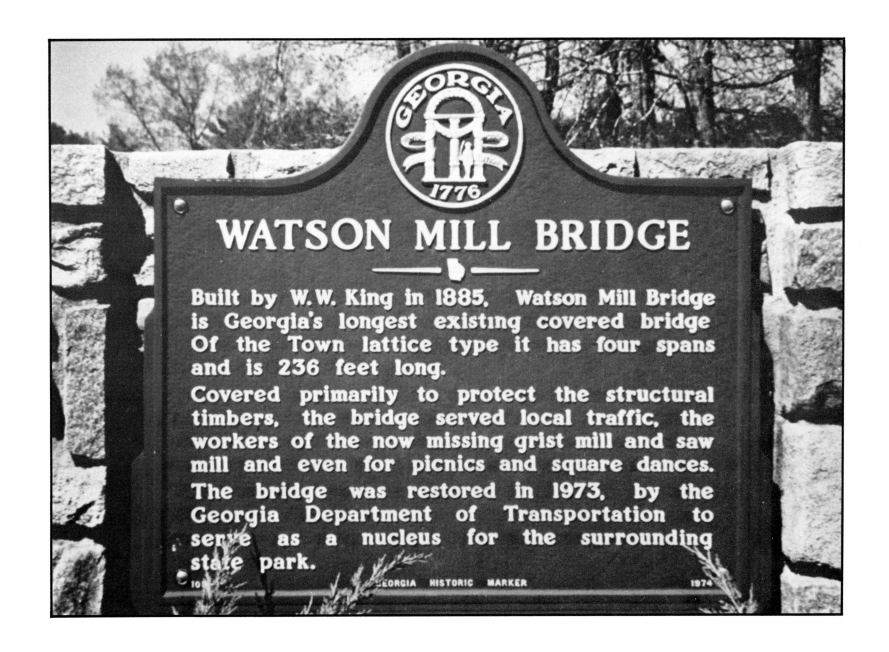

WATSON MILL BRIDGE

Built by W.W. King in 1885, Watson Mill Bridge is Georgia's longest existing covered bridge Of the Town lattice type it has four spans and is 236 feet long.

Covered primarily to protect the structural timbers, the bridge served local traffic, the workers of the now missing grist mill and saw mill and even for picnics and square dances.

The bridge was restored in 1973, by the Georgia Department of Transportation to serve as a nucleus for the surrounding state park.

Because of their beauty or historical value, some are allowed to remain.

Old bridges remind us of other days.

Can you imagine
riding on a horse
through this bridge?

Old bridges allow
only one-way traffic.

New bridges allow many cars at one time.

Bridges are built with strong, durable materials.

Cranes help the builders lift the heavy materials.

Bridges have to be built strong to carry heavy loads.
Some bridges carry railroad tracks and trains.

Bridges have to be built strong to stand up to heavy winds and rapidly moving waters.

Bridges can be built with steel

or with steel and concrete.

Bridges can be built with wood.

Bridges can
even be built
with stones.

Some bridges hang
from strong cables.

Can you find the cables in these pictures?

The strength of a bridge can be reinforced in many ways.
Some bridges have high arches.

Some bridges
have high,
cable-holding
towers.

A bridge's main purpose is to provide passage. But bridges can help in other ways. Bridges can be places for hiding and exploration. Don't forget to look under bridges.

When you walk under a bridge, you might find the homes of mud daubers, spiders or swallows. Barnacles and clams may also live there.

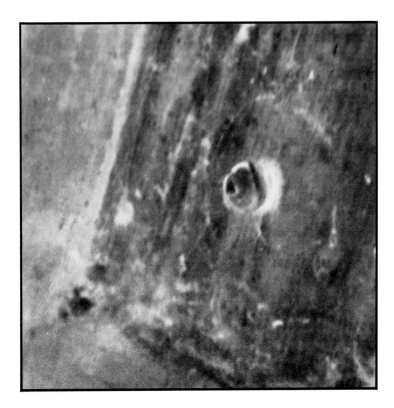

Ducks may paddle around in a bridge's shadow.

Bridges can provide safety from traffic.

They can provide
shelter from the sun.

Bridges work for us under all kinds of conditions.

They bear their load in the sun

and in the rain.

They are there in the ice and snow.

They are there in the fog.

Bridges work in the daytime

and they are busy at night-time.

Look for bridges.

Look carefully
at bridges.

Almost all bridges are beautiful.

The end.

Printed on Paloma Coated Matte — Univers Typeface
Hancock Printing Service, Ellensburg, Washington

Reinforced Binding
Lincoln & Allen, Portland, Oregon

INDEX OF BRIDGES

Names and Locations

( ) indicates highway